Searchlight BOOKS™

Discover Planets

Discover

Mars

Georgia Beth

Lerner Publications ◆ Minneapolis

Lerner Publications Company
A division of Lerner Publishing Group, Inc.
241 First Avenue North
Minneapolis, MN 55401 USA

For reading levels and more information, look up this title
at www.lernerbooks.com.

Main body text set in Adrianna Regular 14/20.
Typeface provided by Chank.

Library of Congress Cataloging-in-Publication Data

Names: Beth, Georgia, author.
Title: Discover Mars / Georgia Beth.
Description: Minneapolis : Lerner Publications, [2018] | Series: Searchlight books.
    Discover planets | Audience: Ages 8–11. | Audience: Grades 4 to 6. | Includes
    bibliographical references and index.
Identifiers: LCCN 2017060842 (print) | LCCN 2017053417 (ebook) |
    ISBN 9781541525436 (eb pdf) | ISBN 9781541523388 (lb : alk. paper) |
    ISBN 9781541527867 (pb : alk. paper)
Subjects: LCSH: Mars (Planet)—Juvenile literature. | Mars (Planet)—Exploration—
    Juvenile literature.
Classification: LCC QB641 (print) | LCC QB641 .B4745 2018 (ebook) |
    DDC 523.43—dc23

LC record available at https://lccn.loc.gov/2017060842

Manufactured in the United States of America
1-44411-34670-2/14/2018

Contents

Chapter 1

THE RED PLANET

Mars has captured our imaginations throughout history. It appears as a bright red light in the sky. It's an alien place. But we long to know more about it.

In ancient times, people thought it was the god of war. As early as 400 BCE, ancient Babylonians studied astronomy. They called the planet Nergal, after the god of death and warfare.

Ancient Romans named Mars (*lower right*) in honor of their god of war.

THERE HAVE BEEN TWENTY-THREE
FAILED MISSIONS, THREE PARTIALLY
SUCCESSFUL MISSIONS, AND EIGHTEEN
SUCCESSFUL MISSIONS TO MARS.

After Earth, Mars is the planet we know the most about. It's a terrestrial planet, meaning it's rocky and has a hard surface. Yet understanding this world isn't easy. Mars is too far away for people to travel there safely. Space programs have sent robot missions to explore the atmosphere and surface of Mars, but many have failed. So there's still much we don't know about Mars.

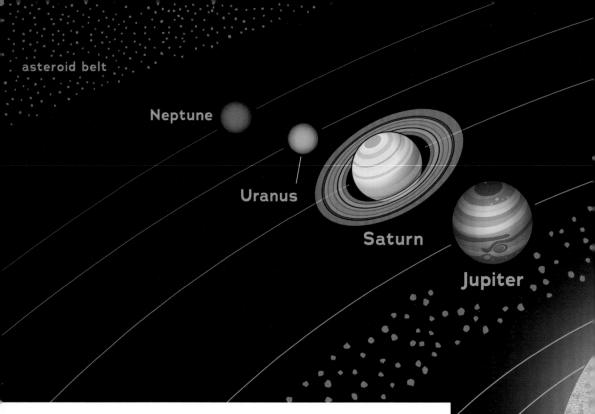

asteroid belt

Neptune

Uranus

Saturn

Jupiter

Earth is the third planet from the sun, and Mars is the fourth. Mars is about 142 million miles (229 million km) from the sun. Though Mars is technically our neighbor, it's still far away. On average, Earth and Mars are about 140 million miles (225 million km) apart.

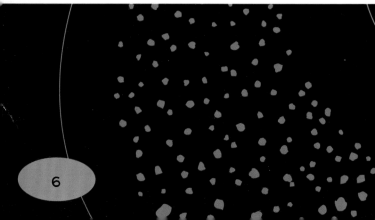

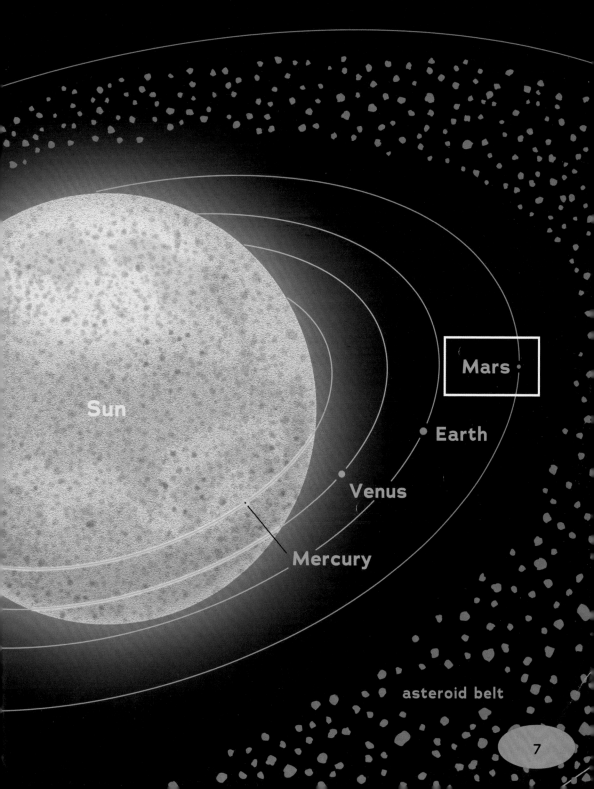

The Solar System

Mars

Earth

Sun

Venus

Mercury

asteroid belt

STEM Highlight

The US National Aeronautics and Space Administration (NASA) plans to send people to Mars as soon as the 2030s. NASA's Office of Planetary Protection researches how to keep robots and astronauts that visit other planets free of bacteria. Bacteria can survive nearly everywhere, so it's not an easy job. Why go to all this trouble? Because bacteria that is harmless to us could hurt life on another planet. And if we ever discover life on Mars, we want to make sure it's Martian and didn't come from Earth!

Scientists at NASA wear protective suits when working on equipment that will travel into space.

Chapter 2

ROCKY AND DUSTY

Mars is small and rocky. At 4,220 miles (6,791 km) wide, Mars is about half the size of Earth. Because of that, Mars has less gravity than Earth.

Mars is also very cold, with an average temperature of –81°F (–63°C). The atmosphere is thin and doesn't provide much protection from asteroids and comets. So the ground is covered in craters. The air is mostly carbon dioxide. That means you can't breathe the air on Mars.

The sunsets on Mars appear an eerie shade of blue.

The surface of the planet is covered in a fine red dust that's rich in rusted iron. There's also a coating of gray volcanic rock on the ground. Avalanches of dust sweep down from the mountains. Huge tornadoes of red powder race across the surface.

The dust storms on Mars are so powerful the entire planet can be coated with a new layer of dust in just a few days.

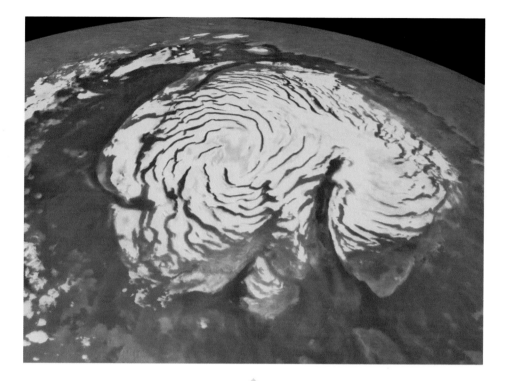

EVIDENCE OF DRY RIVERBEDS, LAKES, AND EVEN OCEANS SUGGESTS THAT MARS MAY HAVE HAD LIQUID WATER ON ITS SURFACE.

Despite its dusty landscape, Mars has water in the form of thick layers of ice at the poles. Along with water ice, there's frozen carbon dioxide. The northern ice cap is surrounded by sand dunes. Images from probes suggest it's a cold desert.

The Tharsis bulge is an area that rises from Mars's surface like a round dome. It's nearly 5,000 miles (8,046 km) wide. Olympus Mons, the largest volcano in the solar system, is found there. It rises 16 miles (26 km) over the ground. Eruptions from Olympus Mons and other volcanoes in the Tharsis region have caused cracks across much of the planet. Some scientists even say the entire Tharsis bulge is one big volcano. That's an idea that's sure to blow anyone's mind!

The other volcanoes in the Tharsis bulge are called Ascraeus Mons, Pavonis Mons, and Arsia Mons.

Phobos and Deimos

Two moons orbit Mars. Phobos is about 14 miles (22 m) wide and orbits three times in a Martian day. Its path is slowly coming closer to the planet. Researchers think it may crash into Mars one day. Deimos is about 8 miles (13 km) across and looks like a potato. It's slowly drifting away from the planet. Both moons are lumpy and long. They can be seen in the sky at the same time from the surface of Mars.

MARS IS THE ONLY TERRESTRIAL
PLANET IN OUR SOLAR SYSTEM THAT
HAS MORE THAN ONE MOON.

STEM Highlight

The northern hemisphere of Mars is mostly smooth, low plains. The southern hemisphere is home to lots of craters and hills. Sound lopsided? You're right! Walking from the North Pole to the South Pole would be one steep climb. In fact, you would pretty much be walking uphill the whole way!

A hemisphere is one of the two halves of a planet.

Landing

What would it be like to live on Mars? No one knows for sure, but it's clear that the lower gravity would have effects on us. Astronauts could have fun bouncing around like a pogo stick, but the low gravity could do some serious damage to human bodies. And health problems would be hard for astronauts to treat. If something did go wrong, it would take fifteen minutes just to send a message from Mars to Earth. That's one of the reasons a trip to Mars would be dangerous for astronauts.

Living with lower gravity could cause people illnesses or injuries.

Chapter 3

STUDYING OUR NEIGHBOR

In 1609, Italian astronomer Galileo Galilei was the first person to observe Mars through a telescope. In 1877, an American astronomer named Asaph Hall was the first to see Phobos and Deimos orbiting Mars. That same year, astronomer Giovanni Schiaparelli mapped light and dark areas of the planet.

Giovanni Schiaparelli was an Italian astronomer.

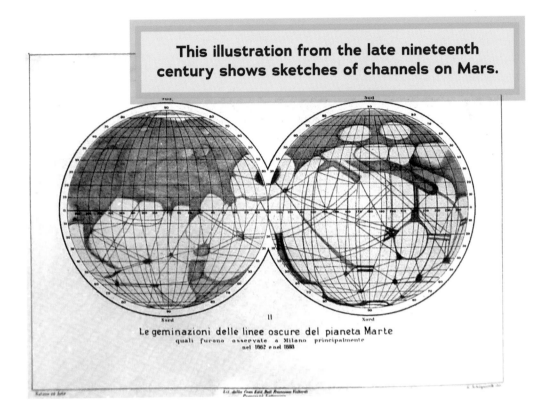

This illustration from the late nineteenth century shows sketches of channels on Mars.

Le geminazioni delle linee oscure del pianeta Marte
quali furono osservate a Milano principalmente
nel 1882 e nel 1888

Schiaparelli also saw deep trenches and grooves in the land that he called *canali* in Italian, or "channels." *Canali* was later mistranslated into English as "canals." Channels are natural features, but canals are human-made waterways. The mistake caused millions of people to imagine aliens building a complex world on Mars.

Later, scientists proved the canals are not actually there. They may have been a trick of the eye or may have even been astronomers seeing the veins of their own eyeballs reflected in their telescopes. But the planet continued to interest people.

VALLES MARINERIS IS NEARLY TEN TIMES AS LONG AS THE GRAND CANYON.

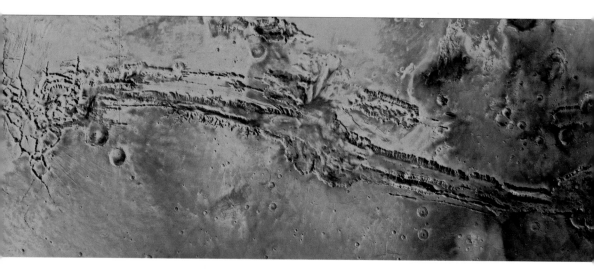

In the 1960s, the Soviet Union, a former group of republics including Russia, tried to send probes to Mars. The United States did too. But those missions failed. Then, in 1971, the Soviet Union's *Mars 3* lander touched down on the planet. It was able to send back only twenty seconds of video before shutting down. Scientists don't know why the probe shut down. That same year, NASA's *Mariner 9* orbited the planet. It sent back images of the two moons. It also took photos of Valles Marineris, an enormous canyon.

In 1975, NASA launched the Viking mission. Two probes, *Viking 1* and *Viking 2*, carried landers designed to search for signs of life on Mars. While they didn't find any life, they did send back data about the weather. They also provided color photographs. These photographs helped scientists see just how red the planet really is. Researchers are still studying data from the Viking mission.

This photo was taken by *Viking 1.*

STEM Highlight

In 1984, a strange meteorite was found in Antarctica. This rock from Mars inspired people to learn more about the planet. Scientists are still debating what it means. The rock is old—likely four billion years old! Some researchers think it carries fossils from Mars. Others say the marks on the meteorite are too small to be proof of life. Scientists are still not sure, but they are studying the meteorite very carefully, hoping this small piece of Mars can help them understand the entire planet.

Some scientists have said they see fossils inside the meteorite that look like tiny worms.

The Next Generation

People didn't launch any other successful missions to Mars until 1996, when NASA sent the *Mars Global Surveyor* to orbit the planet. And a year later, NASA's Pathfinder mission brought the rover *Sojourner* to the red planet.

Sojourner was the first robot with wheels to land on Mars.

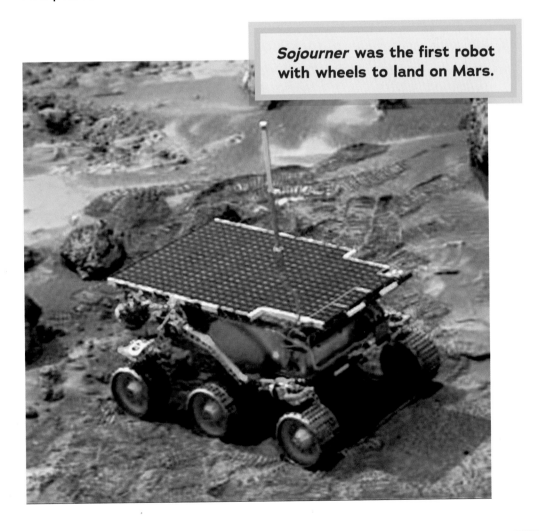

There is so much more that scientists want to learn about Mars. To make the most of each mission, they design new rovers to go farther and learn more. The rovers *Spirit* and *Opportunity* landed on Mars in 2004. *Spirit* lasted for six years, sending back information about the soil and features of the planet.

Opportunity continues to explore the planet and send back data to NASA researchers.

Chapter 4

PUSHING TOWARD THE FUTURE

In 2012, scientists took a new step toward understanding Mars. NASA's *Curiosity* rover landed successfully on the planet. It was designed to find out if there has ever been life on Mars.

The rover could do everything from shooting lasers at rock samples to taking photographs using cutting-edge technology. Most important, it could analyze soil and rock samples. Scientists were excited when the rover found tiny building blocks of life in the samples. The results prove that the red planet has many of the ingredients needed for life.

Curiosity took samples of powdered rock made from the rover's drill.

What's Next

Curiosity is still sending back images and information. And researchers at NASA are considering new ways to learn more about the red planet. Continuing to send probes, rovers, and other machines is a popular option. They can do dangerous work. But they're slow, and we have to control them from far away. Sending humans to the planet would solve these problems. But unlike machines, humans need water, food, and air to survive.

We may soon find out exactly what it would take to survive on Mars. *InSight*, the next spacecraft headed to Mars, is scheduled to launch in 2018. It will study what lies underground. The data it sends back may help scientists understand how rocky planets formed, including Earth. NASA has plans to send another rover to Mars in 2020 before sending humans there in the 2030s.

This artwork shows how *InSight* will explore beneath the surface of Mars.

Living on Mars

Being able to live permanently on Mars one day
would mean humans would need to adapt to the new
environment to survive. Future generations might even
evolve into a new species! Lower levels of gravity would
make bones weaker and more likely to break, so in
response, future humans living on Mars might begin to
develop thicker bones. Pregnancy and giving birth may be
more difficult with less gravity. Because the atmosphere
on Mars is very thin, scientists would have to come up
with better ways to protect humans from the sun's
dangerous rays.

The Big Questions

In the coming years, NASA wants to answer some big questions about Mars. Has there ever been life there? How was the planet formed? How has it changed? And most exciting, can humans live there? One thing is for certain: to answer these questions, we'll need money, time, and creativity. We might even need your help!

NASA's mission to explore, research, and someday send people to the red planet is called Journey to Mars.

STEM Highlight

NASA posted a challenge for people to imagine how humans could live on Mars. People came up with some really creative solutions. Some proposed building colonies underground. Someone else suggested tubes or futuristic igloos. The contest even produced an idea inspired by clamshells.

What do you think would make a good home for Martians?

Looking Ahead

- The first people to live on Mars will need to grow their own food. Algae is easy to transport and grow, so humans on Mars could be eating it for breakfast, lunch, and dinner.

- In 2015, NASA announced they were looking for eight to fourteen people to join missions like Journey to Mars. Over eighteen thousand people applied to join the 2017 astronaut class, but only twelve were chosen. They might be the first people to land on Mars!

- The *Curiosity* rover has artificial intelligence technology that lets it make decisions without human help.

- Billionaire Elon Musk wants to retire on Mars. Would you want to move to the red planet?

Glossary

algae: small plants without roots or stems that grow mainly in water

astronomy: the study of stars, planets, and space

atmosphere: the gases that surround a planet

bacteria: single-celled forms of life

fossil: a bone, shell, or other trace of an animal or plant from millions of years ago that has been turned into rock

gravity: the attraction of one object to another

meteorite: a piece of rock from space that has fallen to Earth

orbit: to travel around another object in an oval or circular path

pole: the end of an invisible straight line a planet rotates around

probe: a device used to explore outer space

solar system: a group consisting of a star and the planets and other objects that orbit the star. In our solar system, the star is the sun.

species: a category of living things that are related and can reproduce

terrestrial planet: a rocky planet

Learn More about Mars

Books

Aldrin, Buzz. *Welcome to Mars: Making a Home on the Red Planet.*
Washington, DC: National Geographic, 2015. Written by one of the
first people to walk on the moon, this book inspires young Earthlings
to imagine what it will be like to live on Mars.

Carney, Elizabeth. *Mars: The Red Planet.* Washington, DC: National
Geographic Kids, 2016. Study the rocks, rovers, and pioneers that
have made this planet so fascinating.

Silverman, Buffy. *Mars Missions: A Space Discovery Guide.* Minneapolis:
Lerner Publications, 2017. Learn more about NASA's efforts to study
Mars and what's needed to send astronauts there.

Websites

All about Mars
https://spaceplace.nasa.gov/all-about-mars/en/
Find more information about Mars, our solar system, and the rest of
the universe on this NASA website.

Mars
https://www.brainpop.com/science/space/mars/
Learn more about Mars as you watch a video, take quizzes, and face
challenges, and more at this fun website.

Mars for Kids
https://mars.nasa.gov/participate/funzone/
Visit this NASA website to play games, find out what you would
weigh on Mars, build a rover, and more.

Index

Photo Acknowledgments

The images in this book are used with the permission of: Giuseppe Parinisi/Shutterstock.com, p. 4; NASA/JPL/Cornell, p. 5; Laura Westlund/Independent Picture Service, pp. 6–7; NASA/KSC, p. 8; NASA/JPL-Caltech/MSSS/Texas A&M Univ., p. 9; NASA/JPL-Caltech/MSSS, pp. 10, 11, 23, 24; NASA/JPL/USGS, pp. 12, 15, 18, 19; NASA/JPL-Caltech/GSFC/Univ. of Arizona, p. 13; NASA/JPL-Caltech/Univ. of Arizona, p. 14; Mondadori Portfolio/Getty Images, p. 16; Giovanni Schiaparelli/Wikimedia Commons (PD), p. 17; NASA/JPL, pp. 20, 21; NASA/JPL/Cornell University/Maas Digital, p. 22; NASA/JPL-Caltech, pp. 25, 27; NASA/JPL-Caltech/Cornell Univ./Arizona State Univ., p. 26.

Front cover: NASA/JPL.